Pittsburgh

Views in the 21st Century

ORIGINAL
Pittsburgh: Views between the Rivers, 1991

UPDATED & EXPANDED
Pittsburgh: Views into the 21st Century, 1996

PUBLISHED 2004
Pittsburgh: Views in the 21st Century
by J. B. Jeffers Ltd.
85 South 34th Street
Boulder, Colorado 80305

PRINTED IN CHINA
by Everbest Printing Company
through Four Colour Imports, Ltd.
Louisville, Kentucky, USA

LIBRARY OF CONGRESS
CONTROL NUMBER: 2004092726

ISBN 0-914355-27-9

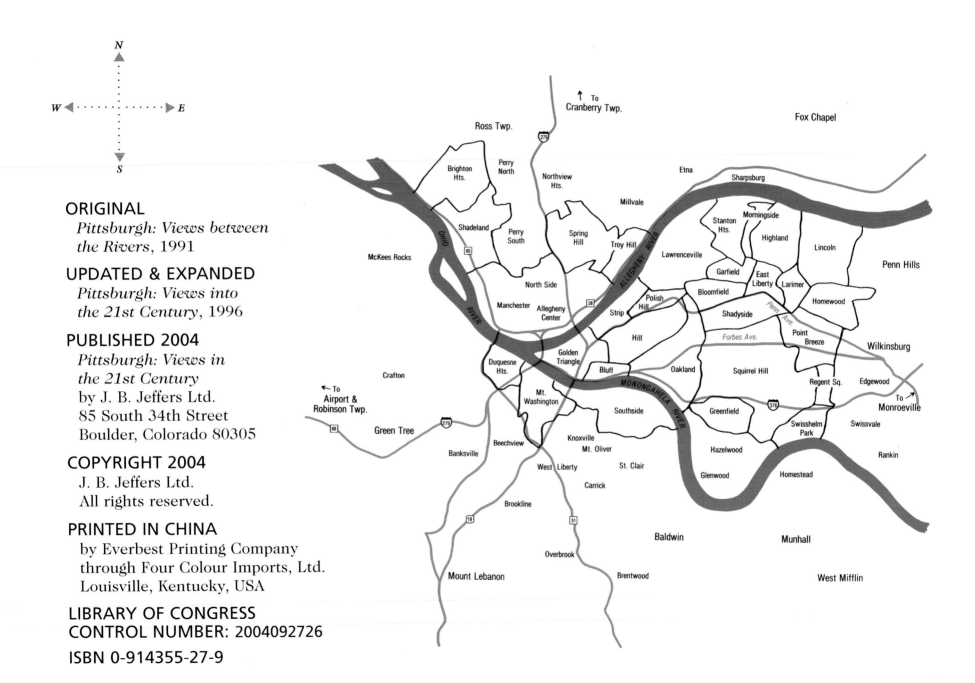

Pittsburgh
Views in the 21st Century

PHOTOGRAPHY
Joel B. Levinson, Susan L. Nega, Richard Kolson,
Norm Schumm, John Beale, Annie O'Neill,
Drew Levinson & Dan Amberson

INTRODUCTION & CAPTIONS
Robert Gangewere & Joel B. Levinson

FRONT & BACK COVER PHOTOGRAPHY
Joel B. Levinson

Joel B. Levinson

Pittsburgh *Views in the 21st Century*

Pittsburgh is a city with a story to tell; photographers, artists and travelers see that immediately. The city is visually exciting and has had a dramatic history, having played a heroic part in the American Industrial Age. Starting after World War II and continuing to this day, an amazing renaissance has transformed this smokey mill town into a city admired for the quality of its urban life.

Arriving in Pittsburgh from the west, the traveler comes through the Fort Pitt Tunnel and immediately confronts a cityscape that leaps to the eye. Apparent at a glance is Pittsburgh's reason for existence: the three rivers which made it an 18th-, 19th-, and 20th-century transportation hub. The Iron City of the 19th century became the Steel City of the post-Civil War era into the 20th century. Pittsburgh's many bridges reveal a history of engineering, design, and construction, and its hills and valleys contain the stories of its ethnic populations.

Now in the 21st century, the vigor and excitement of the area are built around its people and the strengths they have developed through a positive educational, technical, medical, arts, and recreational environment. The modern city, erected on the site of the world's most famous mill town, tells the story of a partnership of citizens, government and private industry redirecting the city's economic energy and literally changing the look of the city.

The Pittsburgh experience for a visitor, however brief, has several levels. First is the surprise of arrival as the city emerges in the arches of the Fort Pitt Bridge as one leaves the Fort Pitt Tunnel. Second, there is the city, highly concentrated 19th century buildings blending in with post-modern architecture. The city fans out from what is known as the "Golden Triangle" to the neighborhoods, marked by old-world churches and ethnic stability.

Pittsburgh's second city is the Oakland area, with its museums, educational and medical facilities, and the large Schenley Park, with a pool, skating rink, conservatory, golf course and trails. Oakland will also boast the first robot museum, the Robot Hall of Fame. The pleasures of the city abound in Oakland, on the hill tops and in the hidden valleys.

With its interesting cityscapes, neighborhood and citywide events, cultural and historic treasures, Pittsburgh has become a Mecca for the millions throughout adjoining Pennsylvania, West Virginia and Ohio communities, as well as national and international travelers. The photographs in this book capture the pace and variety of the community so many have come to love.

— Robert Gangewere & Joel B. Levinson

View of Pittsburgh coming into the city through the Fort Pitt Tunnel

Joel B. Levinson

5

Sunrise launch of hot air balloons over the city

As the sun sets, the city takes on a golden glow.

Joel B. Levinson

7

8

Coming into the City

J oin us in exploring a view between the rivers as seen from its many approaches. For many people living on Mount Washington, with its most spectacular views of the city, the two inclines, Monongahela and Duquesne, are more than just the city's biggest attractions – they are a way to get to work.

Joel B. Levinson

The city from the east. Gone are the steel mills (page 97) that sprawled along the Monongahela River, replaced by the new technology center complex.

The city magically appears from the south and west during a trip through Fort Pitt tunnels.

From the west along the Ohio River, the city is framed by the majestic arches of the West End Bridge.

Susan L. Nega

Coming from the north, the interstate snakes through the city's many hills and valleys. Eventually the city appears in all its grandeur, behind and around the 2003 winged roof of the newly renovated Convention Center.

Light Rail Transit becomes subway in the Golden Triangle.

Port Authority Light Rail Transit exiting the city

Both photos, Joel B. Levinson

13

There are numerous choices when deciding on how to reach the city, as a commuter or as a visitor. Whether one chooses train, bus, car, barge, light rail transit, river boat, airplane, or hot air balloon, the traveler is always welcomed to the rivers' outstretched arms with exciting vistas.

Pittsburgh International Airport

The airport is located 20 miles west of the Golden Triangle. It is the most unique airport in the country, and at the time it was built it was considered years ahead of itself. The midfield terminal is in the shape of an "X," with a shopping mall of boutique stores at the center. The midfield terminal connects to the main landside terminal by an underground people-mover. The airport and city are linked by the parkway west and a limited-access busway.

Joel B. Levinson

Susan L. Nega

15

Lets Take a Balloon or a Parachute into the City

Many people might prefer arriving by a hot air balloon, but service hasn't been initiated yet and probably never will. However, that doesn't stop thousands from flocking to the Point each year, especially during the Regatta mania, to watch them lift off by the dozens (page 6). Because of the hills and river valleys, the air flow can send the balloons north one day, south the next, and east an hour later any day. The summer Regatta brings to the Point many other travelers, like the sky diver pictured here.

Here Come the Barges

Barges were Pittsburgh's main lifeline during the 19th and 20th centuries. Even today they are a vital industrial link, bringing in coal, gas, sand, gravel, and occasionally the odd cargo, like the submarine for the Carnegie Science Center.

Both photos, Joel B. Levinson

17

The City

No matter how you come to the city, you will find its magic. It is a blend of antique structures dwarfed by modern, tall skyscrapers housing corporate offices, law firms, financial institutions and services, telecommunications companies, technology firms, hotels, a convention center, regional and federal courts, and numerous philanthropic offices. The city center is often referred to as the Golden Triangle and encompasses a very compact space nestled between the rivers and hills. However, most feel the city's footprint extends to the north and south shores.

The city center's vitality partially originates from the cultural establishments located there, including the symphony, ballet, the public theater, art galleries, the Andy Warhol Museum, the Carnegie Science Center, and the Pittsburgh Regional History Center.

Joel B. Levinson

The changing Pittsburgh cityscape is dynamic and even those Pittsburghers who have lived through the constantly changing detours, motoring interruptions, and delays do not recognize the city that has emerged. From the West End Overlook at the city's north shore, the two new stadiums appear behind the Carnegie Science Center, the yellow 6th (renamed Roberto Clemente Memorial Bridge), 7th, and 9th Street bridges, and the roof wings of the newly completed Convention Center.

An illuminated Smithfield Street Bridge (1883) leads from Station Square to a city alive with lights.

Visual treasures of the changing city skyline appear from the roadways leading down from the hills along the Monongahela River's south shore.

Both photos,, Joel B. Levinson

20

Joel B. Levinson

The city is filled with commanding veiws. Tourists generally favor Mount Washington, but about a mile down the Ohio, at a turnoff to the West End Overlook, is a vista that is unequaled. This view captures the new city as it starts the 21st century.

Smithfield United Church (1925)

The steeples of Pittsburgh's churches have influenced the modern architecture of the city's newer, more prominent structures, such as the PPG building and Fifth Avenue Place.

Trinity Episcopal

St. John Ukranian Church (1895), South Side

All photos, Joel B. Levinson

22

Susan L. Nega

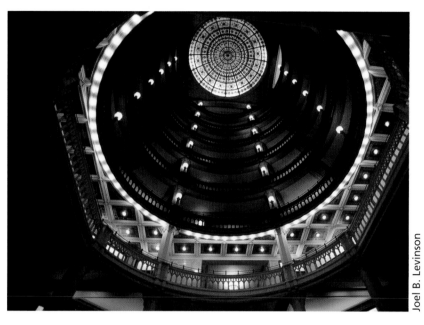

Joel B. Levinson

*Foyer and atrium at
Two Mellon Bank Center,
formerly Union Trust Building*

Joel B. Levinson

*Fort Pitt Blockhouse
(1794) in Point
State Park*

Mellon Square

Joel B. Levinson

23

Point State Park fountain, the city's focal point

Kaufman's Clock, a favorite meeting place at the corner of 5th and Smithfield Streets

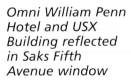

Courthouse steps with a sculpture of the late Mayor Richard Caliguiri, the driving force behind the 1980s renaissance

Omni William Penn Hotel and USX Building reflected in Saks Fifth Avenue window

Golden Triangle from the north shore

Sparkling Gateway building with Fifth Avenue Place in the background

25

Northlight Sculpture by D. Von Schlegell in front of the Oxford Building

Northlight sculpture by D. Von Schlegell in front of the Oxford Building

1900 wharf buildings on Fort Pitt Boulevard (see page 101)

Duquesne University, sitting on top of the bluff overlooking the Golden Triangle

The 10th Street suspension bridge connects the South Side to the Armstrong tunnels beneath Duquesne University campus.

Pittsburgh's downtown is an easy walk, enjoyable because one encounters its wonders and its history. Take the underground subway and one misses many of the city's nooks and crannies, such as the Liberty Avenue historic-cultural district, or the 18th-century cemetery along Oliver street, or H. H. Richardson's 1888 Allegheny Courthouse gardens. Foyers like the one at Alcoa's new headquarters, just across the 9th Street Bridge, and intimate small parks like the one adjoining Heinz Hall shouldn't be overlooked.

*1888 Allegheny
Courthouse yard*

*Alcoa Building
foyer (2000)*

Early 1900s building along Liberty Avenue

Joel B. Levinson

Joel B. Levinson

Susan L. Nega

28

Pittsburgh is the "City of Bridges," and in its Golden Triangle they are yellowish-gold.

Joel B. Levinson

29

The Carnegie Science Center, Heinz Football Stadium, and Allegheny Hospital on the city's North Side, viewed from Mount Washington

The Bridge of Sighs connects the 1888 Allegheny Courthouse and its jail, recently renovated into an office-exhibit complex.

Any view of the Golden Triangle features the skyscraper known to all as the PPG Building. Its glass walls reflecting its surroundings, the PPG tower is the focal point of the other PPG buildings, which enclose a courtyard alive with activity and year-round fun. During the winter the courtyard is converted into a skating rink. In the summer the courtyard encourages visitors to throw off their shoes and dance among the illuminated water jets.

Oakland, Pittsburgh's Second City

Oakland is home to Pittsburgh's two largest universities, world-renowned medical centers, cultural attractions, apartment and residential living, and Schenley Park, a four-season experience. The Oakland area developed around the end of the 19th century when Mary Schenley gave the city the park that bears her name. Andrew Carnegie stepped forward with the Carnegie Museum, the Free Library, and Carnegie Institute of Technology, now Carnegie Mellon University. Phipps added the Conservatory (1893), which has flower shows year-round. Just two of the area's hundreds of attractions are the "Original," nationally acclaimed for its hot dogs, and Dippy the Dinosaur, shown here, welcoming visitors to the museum's massive collection.

33

Schenley Park – Oakland's and the City's Year-round Playground

Westinghouse Memorial in Schenley Park

Joel B. Levinson

Susan L. Nega

Schenley Park skating rink

Phipps Conservatory during the Christmas holidays

Joel B. Levinson

34

Phipps Conservatory (1893) features botanical displays and four seasonal flower shows.

Joel B. Levinson

The library, museum and two of Oakland's universities have Schenley Park as part of their open space. Winter activities include cross-country skiing, sled riding and ice skating, while sunny periods bring out golfers, sun bathers, academics, and those enjoying events that use the park as part of their venue.

Joel B. Levinson

Joel B. Levinson

Susan L. Nega

Joel B. Levinson

36

The Carnegie

The Carnegie, a great natural history museum, art gallery, and library complex founded by Andrew Carnegie in 1895, is the focal point of the Oakland area. Outside the entrance to this palace of culture are symbolic sculptures, including those of Shakespeare and Galileo.

Part of the Carnegie is located on Pittsburgh's North Side, where the Andy Warhol Museum (page 55) and the Science Center (page 53) are housed.

Sculpture Hall, with special exhibit

Museum and Scafe Gallery entrance

All photos, Joel B. Levinson

Explore the Carnegie

The exciting museum and art gallery exhibits are numerous and constantly changing. Permanent collections like the one in the dinosaur hall have featured interactive robots and now have several hands-on exhibits. At Christmas time, the architecture hall features decorated trees, concerts, and choral groups. The Sarah Scafe Art Gallery has many wonderful pieces in the permanent collection but also feature traveling exhibits. Once every three years the gallery hosts the Carnegie International. Hidden treasures are the Carnegie Music Hall and the grand, marble entry hall. Behind the museum exhibits on the first floor is the six hundred-seat Carnegie Lecture Hall, where Andy Warhol took classes with other Pittsburgh youngsters showing artistic talent.

Norm Schumm

Carnegie Mellon University (CMU)

CMU's campus is shown on the previous page. For decades, CMU has been internationally recognized as the educational and research leader in technical and management curricula in the fields of civil, chemical, mechanical engineering, architecture and applied sciences. Over the last two decades, Carnegie Mellon also has gained recognition as one of the foremost universities in computer science and robotics. Beyond technology, the drama, music, art and humanities departments have many entertainers, art celebrities, and dignitaries on their alumni rosters.

CMU buggy races

Margaret Morrison Building

Hamerschlag Hall (1912) and Wean Hall Computer Center

All photos, Joel B. Levinson

40

Track at CMU's
Gesling Stadium

Porter Hall
foyer

Mellon Institute houses biological offices and research labs.

Sketching at the
Fine Arts Building

Olympic swimming pool
at the Student Union

All photos, Joel B. Levinson

41

Between the city's two most prestigious universities is Craig Street. Just across from the entrance to the Carnegie's Sarah Scafe Gallery, it is few-block area filled with unique retail establishments selling clothing, rare books, cards and gifts, comic books, art, jewelry, and drafting-artist supplies, and restaurants with diverse ethnic menus.

Watermelon Blues

John Beale

Caliban Books

Joel B. Levinson

Joel B. Levinson

Craig Street shops

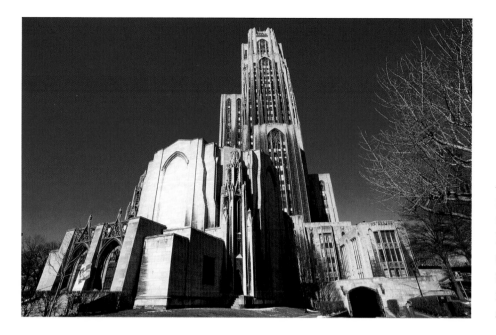

University of Pittsburgh

A landmark seen from almost all of Pittsburgh's neighborhoods, the University's 42-floor-high Cathedral of Learning (page 101) dominates the local landscape. It nationally and internationally signifies the home of acclaimed educational schools that service the medical-dental practices and research, legal, library science, education, business, and political science disciplines.

In 2001 the beloved Pitt Stadium made way for the Peterson Event Center at right.

Studying inside the Cathedral of Learning

Sled riding in front of Heinz Chapel on campus

The English Classroom, one of the nationality rooms in the Cathedral

University of Pittsburgh's Cathedral of Learning

Reflections in Mervis Hall, location of the Joseph M. Katz Graduate School of Business

The cultural district's Harris Theater,
showing special art movies

*Benedum Center
for Performing Arts*

*Mellon Arena during a special
program, with its dome open
to expose the city skyline*

City Attractions

Throughout the City and its environs, numerous attractions beckon the surrounding population. Events such as those accompanying the July 4th fireworks and concerts at the Point bring in many. Downtown attractions include the ballet, symphony, theater, other performing arts, and the remnants of the 18th century Fort Pitt battlements and block house. Across the Allegheny River are the Andy Warhol Museum, Carnegie Science Center, National Aviary, Children's Museum, Carnegie's first free library, and the Allegheny Observatory. Immediately across the Monongahela River is the Station Square Complex and the two remaining inclines. Stretching eastward is Kennywood Amusement Park, the Frick Art and Historical Center, Pittsburgh Zoo, Sand Castles, and farther east near Ligonier are Idlewild Amusement Park and Frank Lloyd Wright's Fallingwater.

Fourth of July celebration at the Point

Joel B. Levinson

John Beale

Station Square has changed in the new century with the addition of the Bessemer Court buildings and fountain.

Station Square

Station Square is a favorite spot for visitors and Pittsburghers alike. Built by Pittsburgh Landmarks and Historical Society at the site of the early 20th century P&LERR railroad station and yards, it originally was developed as a retail mall, with the Grand Concourse Restaurant and a major hotel. It is now an office, entertainment, dining, and shopping complex, with many of Pittsburgh's industrial heirlooms on display. Station Square lies just across the historic Smithfield Street Bridge (1883) from the Golden Triangle.

Joel B. Levinson

Monongahela Incline is one way to reach the Station Square complex from Mount Washington.

Joel B. Levinson

The Bessemer converter from one of the Ohio Mills has a new home among other mill equipment throughout the complex.

Station Square, situated across the Monongahela River from the Point, is a place where the visitor has one foot in the city's past and one foot in the high-tech present.

Heinz Hall lobby event

O'Reilley Public Theater

Heinz Hall

Ballet at Benedium Center

On the North Side, the Mattress Factory Museum's "Repetitive Vision" room was created by Yayoi Kusama.

Susan L. Nega

Carnegie Science Center

Located directly across from the confluence of the Allegheny, Monongahela, and Ohio Rivers sits the Carnegie Science Center, with its rooftop sculpture "E-Motion," which changes colors to predict the weather, and where the submarine USS Requin is permanently moored. Here children of all ages can interact with scientific exhibits, see each holiday season a fantastic model train display, and enjoy a movie at Rangos Omnimax Theater.

Learning through interaction

Christmas train display

Allegheny Square

The Pittsburgh Children's Museum is located in the old post office building in Landmark Square, on Pittsburgh's North Side. A sculpture garden adjoins it, featuring historic pieces of Pittsburgh's history including the Portal Sculptures (1915), pictured here, from the Manchester Bridge, which was replaced by the Fort Duquesne Bridge in the 1960s. Every year the Children's Festival is held here and throughout Allegheny Center. The National Aviary is close by in Allegheny West Park.

Susan L. Nega

Susan L. Nega

Joel B. Levinson

Joel B. Levinson

"Silver Clouds"

The Andy Warhol Museum

The Andy Warhol Museum was opened by the Carnegie in 1994. Located on the North Side, it's a short walk across the 9th Street Bridge from the Golden Triangle. The museum features an extensive collection of Warhol's art and archives. A Pittsburgh native, Andy Warhol graduated from Carnegie Institute of Technology (now CMU), worked at the old Horne's department store, and became one of the most influential American artists of the 20th century.

Susan L. Nega

55

The Clayton

The beautifully restored Victorian home of industrialist Henry Clay Frick, the Clayton is part of the Frick Art & Historical Center in the Point Breeze section of Pittsburgh. Also on the grounds are the Frick Art Museum, built in 1969 to house Helen Clay Frick's collection of fine and decorative arts, the Carriage Museum, a greenhouse (a smaller version of Phipps Conservatory in Schenley Park), and the complex's lush gardens.

Susan L. Nega

Dinning room in the Clayton House

The Clayton House

Joel B. Levinson

56

Susan L. Nega

The Pittsburgh Zoo

Nestled on the high ground above the Allegheny River in East Liberty is the Pittsburgh Zoo and Children's Zoo. The grounds have been changed over the years to provide the topography that is more in keeping with the animals' natural habitats. Gone are most of the bars and cages that were characteristic of the early- to mid-20th century. Aquariums, wild bird enclosures, and open spaces make the visitor feel as if he's there in the animals' environment. The Pittsburgh Zoo is rated as one of the top zoos in the country.

Richard Kolson

Richard Kolson

57

Mr. Rogers's neighborhood trolley at Idlewild Park

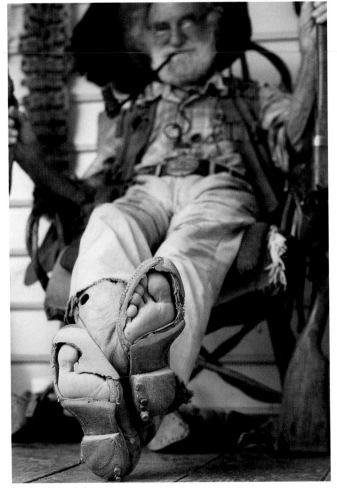

Friendly old codger

Sandcastle Water Park

The world-famous Thunderbolt, a wood-frame rollercoaster

Joel B. Levinson

Raging rapids

Susan L. Nega

Amusement Parks

There are three amusement parks in the area: Kennywood Park in West Mifflin, which traces its history back to a streetcar park around 1900; Sandcastle water park on the Monongahela River in Homestead; and Idlewild Park, about 35 miles east on Route 30 in Ligonier, where kids can have their own park and adults can just enjoy being young again.

Wave Swinger

Joel B. Levinson

59

Pittsburgh Neighborhoods

Pittsburgh neighborhoods radiate in all directions from the Point. Some are tucked along hillsides or in valleys. Some balance precariously atop overlooks, and some border its many parks. Many of them, such as Bloomfield, Polish Hill, and Troy Hill, have strong ethnic backbones that date back generations.

Joel B. Levinson

Homes in Spring HIll and the city's skyscrapers at dusk

Mexican War Street home

North Side

A short ten-minute walk across the golden bridges is Old Allegheny, now known as North Side. Allegheny General Hospital is the focal point of the area. The community college looks down on the new PNC Park and Heinz Field. Houses on the Mexican War streets date back to the late 19th Century. Troy Hill is on the crest of the hill looking down on North Side.

Troy Hill center

Pittsburgh is a city of hills and valleys. So many streets started off paved with cobblestones, and today some still exist. They have become neighborhood icons, jealously protected by the residents.

Joel B. Levinson

South Side hillside

East End homes

East End homes

Polish Hill

From the Ashes of a Steel-making King, a New Complex Emerges

Across the Homestead High Level Bridge from Pittsburgh's Squirrel Hill, the city of Homestead is transforming itself with a new living, office, shopping, and entertainment community. Where steel was king and steelworkers became legends, only the chimneys that serviced the mills' soaking pits remain, preserved as historic markers to the mills' existence and influence on the area and the country.

Joel B. Levinson

John Beale

Joel B. Levinson

The new community of Washington Landing, located on Herr Island, beneath the 31st Street Bridge

John Beale

Shadyside

Shadyside is a 19th-century neighborhood of homes, apartments, and the trendy Walnut Street shopping area. Each year an artisan street fair brings thousands of browsers. In summer, people gather at Mellon Park, which adjoins Shadyside, Squirrel Hill, and Point Breeze, for Bach and Beethoven in a brunch concert series.

Bach, Beethoven and Sunday morning brunch in Mellon Park

Sunday morning on Walnut Street

66

South Side flats and the Birmingham Bridge to Oakland

Joel B. Levinson

Squirrel Hill

Bordered by Schenley and Frick Parks, Squirrel Hill is Pittsburgh's largest neighborhood. Developed in the early 20th century, it is a melting pot of all social, economic, educational, and ethnic-international backgrounds.

The main arteries of Forbes, Murray, and Forward Avenues provide two miles of shopping, eating, and entertainment establishments.

The city's newest neighborhood, Summerset is part of Squirrel HIll and looks over Homestead and Parkway West.

The Mt. Washington neighborhood overlooks the city.

Bloomfield

Bloomfield shines at night along Liberty Avenue. This neighborhood is a strong ethnic community and home to many businesses. It abounds with fine eateries appreciated citywide. Close by on Baum Boulevard, Ritters Diner has been a favorite stop for decades.

Joel B. Levinson

Susan L. Nega

East Liberty

East Liberty is just east of Bloomfield and north of Shadyside. Cantini's "Joy of Life" sculpture (1969) sits outside the neighborhood branch of the Carnegie Library and Presbyterian Cathedral. The library, cathedral, and Motor Square Gardens, in the foreground of the aerial photo, are a short walk from East Liberty Mall.

Joel B. Levinson

Joel B. Levinson

Joel B. Levinson

At South HIgh's Field on Carson Street is a 2003 tribute to the city's high schools.

Technology, Industry and Medicine in Pittsburgh

Pittsburgh grew up as a steel town. With the exception of a steel-continuous casting operation in Braddock, steel-making no longer is part of the city's fibre. When steel was king, Pittsburgh also had the king of ketchup. The Heinz Food Company is still a part of the changing city's life blood. It's slow-pouring ketchup is enshrined in a neon sign at its plant on the North Side near the 16th Street Bridge. Also pictured is Pittsburgh's Technology Center, which has grown up on the site of 2nd Avenue's J & L Blast Furnace (page 96).

Through its strong university research programs, the city has become a center for robotic, medical, biotech and software technology, which has caused high-technology companies to spring up throughout the area. Thirty new biomedical technology ventures have formed since 1996. The sector encompasses 25,000 scientists working in more than 170 research facilities. Pittsburgh's medical facilities and medical research centers are acknowledged internationally as dominant leaders.

All photos, Joel B. Levinson

CMU Robotics Institute

Research at CMU Robotics Institute, in cooperation with the city's medical facilities, including West Penn Hospital, has involved developing new computer-based medical devices and procedures to improve patient outcomes through increased speed and accuracy in surgical procedures. Shown below is a Mars robot being tested on Devon Island in the Arctic by CMU students associated with the Robotics Institute. The Mars project, a jointly sponsored activity, tests numerous practices that might be needed for exploring the Red Planet. The robot, with a CMU spokesperson, is being filmed for a Discovery Channel presentation on the project.

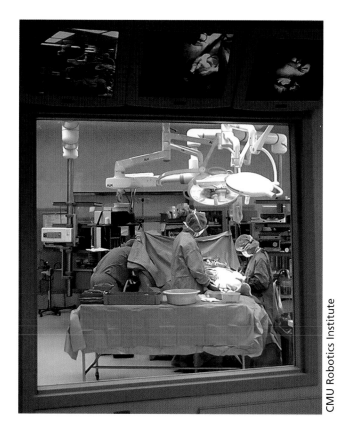

CMU Robotics Institute

Drew Levinson

73

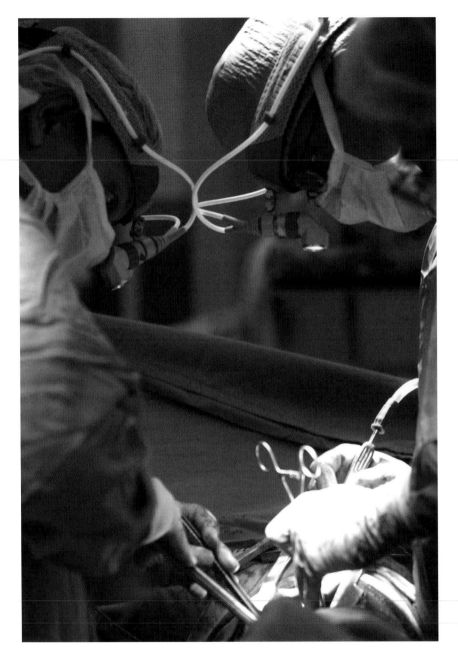
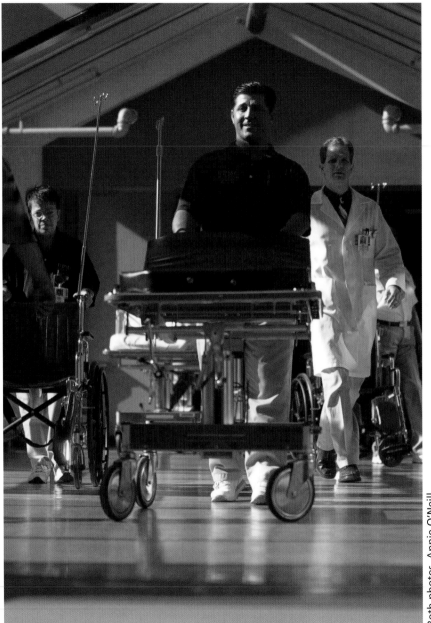

Both photos, Annie O'Neill

Pittsburgh is home to some of the finest health care in the country. The University of Pittsburgh Medical Center (UPMC) is the region's premier health care system and one of the largest in the country. UPMC and its academic partner, the University of Pittsburgh, comprise a leading research center and a source of life-enhancing health care for the region. UPMC includes twenty tertiary care, speciality, and community hospitals, as well as a network of doctors' offices, cancer centers, imaging and surgical facilities, rehabilitation sites, behavioral health care, nursing homes and senior living facilities. Most of the pictures on these two pages were taken at their facilities.

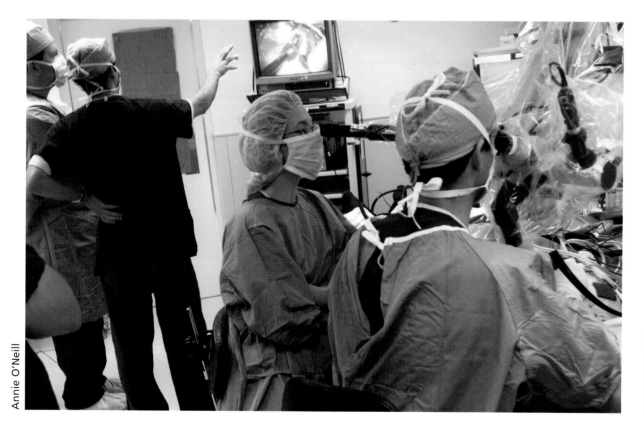

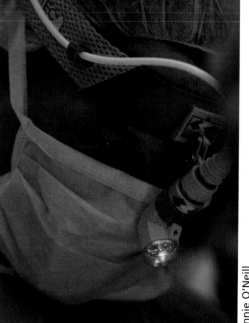

Sports in Pittsburgh

The Steelers

The Steelers and their fans got a new home in 2001. Heinz Field seats a maximum of 64,000 screaming fans. Both the Steelers and the University of Pittsburgh Panthers call it their home turf. Tailgate parties are just part of Steeler mania, as is Myron Cope's "Terrible Towel." The stadium also is used for large concerts and was constructed so everyone can view the scoreboard and also get an unobstructed view of the city.

Joel B. Levinson

Joel B. Levinson

Norman Schumm

The Pirates

The Pittsburgh Pirates have been an institution in Pittsburgh since the early 1900s, when games were played at Exhibition Park, which existed between the new Heinz Field and PNC Park. Pirate fans are everywhere throughout the country. The tattoo on the arm of a postal employee in Boulder, Colorado, shows just how far-reaching and loyal their base is. Reminiscent of the old Forbes Field (page 99), PNC Park, shown below, opened in 2002.

Pittsburgh Pirate Icons

The love of baseball is a natural evolution starting with a childhood adoration of the team's players. PNC Park is a tribute to Pirate athletes throughout the years. Banners of team heroes hang from columns and building steelwork, and three – Honus Wagner, Roberto Clemente and Willie Stargell – have been immortalized with action statues depicted below. Look carefully at the 1970 batter's box photo and you will find Clemente at bat and Stargell in the on-deck circle.

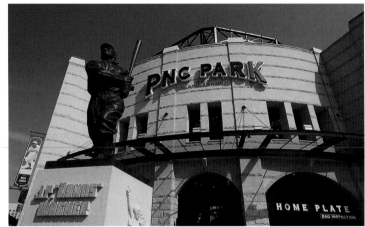

John Beale

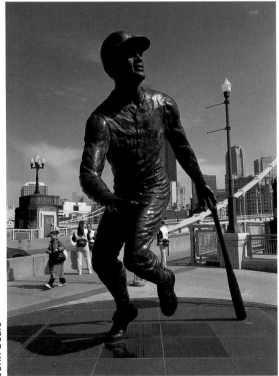

John Beale

Joel B. Levinson

Joel B. Levinson

Pittsburgh Penguins

The Penguins' hockey games are played at Civic Arena.

Joel B. Levinson

Pittsburgh neighborhoods play host to sports enthusiasts. Here the Great Race runs through Squirrel Hill on its way to the finish line in Point State Park.

Joel B. Levinson

One of the fastest growing sports in the area is rowing. Each year the city hosts the Ohio Rowing Regatta. Most crews start from Herrs Island (Washington's Landing) and end at the Point.

Fans offer cheers of support to the Marathon runners as they start up the ramp to the Birmingham Bridge in South Side. They proceed along the neighborhood streets, through the Strip District and then across the Allegheny River on the 16th Street Bridge before making there way to the finish line in Point State Park. The Marathon has been a city favorite for years but will be suspended in 2004, hopefully not for long.

Both photos, Joel B. Levinson

Pittsburgh's Hidden Treasures

Joel B. Levinson

A quiet moment on the north shore looking across the river to downtown Pittsburgh

Three Rivers Art Festival

Every June the festival brings a variety of art to people throughout the Golden Triangle. Invited artist vendors offer sculpture, paintings, photography, and video, while music, dance, food, and fireworks add to the exciting atmosphere.

All photos, Joel B. Levinson

Three Rivers Regatta

This event attracts hundreds of thousands of people from the Tri-State area to play along the banks of Pittsburgh's three rivers. The Formula One races have been the centerpiece of the activity, with hot air balloons and anything-that-floats contests expanding the action. Memorable fireworks close the event.

All photos, Joel B. Levinson

85

The Rotunda

The Rotunda is the gateway to The Pennsylvanian, a complex of offices and residential apartments. These early 20th-century structures, including the railroad loading platforms, were the Pennsylvania Railroad headquarters and its Pennsylvania Union Station. The skylit, grand circular dome has four, arched turret supports, each with medallion destinations – Pittsburgh, New York, Philadelphia, and Washington – dated "1900." The lobby is occasionally used for civic gatherings, weddings, and events (also see page 102).

Dan Kamin,
internationally
acclaimed mime,
with friends
at polo event

All photos, Joel B. Levinson

The Grand Prix event in Schenley Park
brings together sports car enthusiasts
and everyone else from the city and
surrounding communities.

The Strip District

A marketplace of small shops and stands peddling all kinds of sundry items and souvenirs, the Strip indulges those "Pittsburghers" who make it Saturday's day-out destination for fresh produce, meats, fish, pasta, cheeses, ethnic foods, fresh-cut flowers, and ethnic cuisine.

Joel B. Levinson

Joel B. Levinson

Susan L. Nega

Joel B. Levinson

The Jewels of Pittsburgh are Its People

A blend of backgrounds, interests, and lifestyles make Pittsburgh a great place to live. Everyone who has lived in the "Burg" and moved away mentions it first when referring to places and things they miss.

All photos, Joel B. Levinson

89

Reclamation, Celebration, and Spirit

Anyone trying to photographically capture a city as alive, interesting, friendly, and welcoming, and with as rich of a history as Pittsburgh, faces many challenges. First and foremost is: what do you include and what do you pass over, and where do you stop? Reclamation, celebration, and spirit are what this book is all about. Hopefully each page can be appreciated from this perspective.

Joel B. Levinson

The Doughboy sculpture by A. Newman (1921) in Lawrenceville at Penn and Butler Streets, where the Pennsylvanian Bank Building has been converted into an architect's office.

Joel B. Levinson

Fireworks in honor of the New Year's celebration city hosts

Susan L. Nega

There is never a lack of enthusiasm or spirit in this city.

Pittsburgh and Parades, a Love Affair

Similar to the highly successful Macy's Thanksgiving Day Parade in New York City, Pittsburgh's parade kicks off the year-end holiday season with many floats and air-filled caricatures.

Joel B. Levinson

Pittsburgh and Parades, a Love Affair

Organize a parade and the residents come out in droves. Each year the St. Patrick's Day Parade brings out a shivering crowd to cheer on the marchers. Billed as one of the longest parades in the country, no one is ever sure whether the honor is for the distance the marchers travel or the number of marching entries and participants.

The Labor Day Parade, which should carry the same honors as the St. Patrick's Day Parade, was one of the nation's first to commemorate the day.

Labor Day Parade

Labor Day Parade

Both photos, Joel B. Levinson

93

Pittsburghers Walk and Run in Support of Worthwhile Causes

Over the years the "Race for the Cure" has drawn larger and larger crowds. Pittsburgh was one of the first cities to throw its support into raising funds for cancer research. Other similar walks for worthwhile causes are a part of the city fiber, but none draw crowds, upwards of 35,000 people, as this one.

Race for the Cure weaves through Squirrel Hill residential streets.

Race for the Cure runners at the starting line on the Schenley Park golf course

Light-up NIght in the Point State Park

Susan L. Nega

Things Pittsburgh Has Left Behind – a Rich Historical Past

Pittsburgh has grown from an internationally known city of steel and smoke to a pristine oasis with a diverse industrial base, while retaining old world charm from its largely ethnic population. Few of its citizens are still around who can remember those early days, but many fondly remember the things that exemplified the city's transformation.

Susan L. Nega

Thrift Drug Bike Classic died in the late 1990s, but enthusiasts talk of bringing it back.

Joel B. Levinson

Before its removal, the sign from J & L Steel (LTV) glowed in the late afternoon sun on the South Side.

Joel B. Levinson

Klein's, Pittsburgh's once-famous eatery, has its sign and menus preserved with other city memorabilia in the Heinz History Center in the Strip.

Where they lived, where they worked, where they built (1982)

Pittsburgh is the city of bridges – beautiful bridges with accent lighting especially appreciated at night. A bridge-lighting trial was conducted in the late '90s, and now many city devotees wish it had continued on even a limited basis.

Joel B. Levinson

Forbes Field

Forbes Field's centerfield wall has been preserved on the University of Pittsburgh campus. The wall shows a 436-foot marker commemorating the spot where Bill Mazoroski's ball exited for a ninth inning home run. The ball "left the park" and won the 1960 World Series. Also preserved in the walkways and halls on campus are the left field wall and home plate.

When in 2001 PNC Park was built on the Pittsburgh's north shore at the 7th Street Bridge, the architects tried to recreate the baseball experience that Forbes Field gave the fans.

Joel B. Levinson

Harold Corsini

Forbes Field, circa 1953

99

Step Back into Pittsburgh's Past as It Entered the Last Century

The Point, circa 1900, looking westward

The Point, circa 1900, looking eastward

Looking toward the Point over what is now Market Square

Smokey City Beach, circa 1908

Steamboats along the wharf at the Point with Wabash Bridge and 1st Avenue in the background, circa 1915

World War I inductees leaving riverboats and running to trains, circa 1917

1919 tour bus

University of Pittsburgh, 1929

Gathering on Flagstaff Hill, Schenley Park, circa 1905

Pennsylvania Union Railroad Station Rotunda, leading to the Strip District

Acknowledgements

The photographs in this photographic essay on Pittsburgh are primarily those taken by Joel B. Levinson and Susan L. Nega. Together they managed J. B. Jeffers Ltd., which marketed PITTSBURGHSCAPE photographic products such as books, calendars, postcards, tour guides, maps, stock photography, and related products. Though J. B. Jeffers Ltd.'s activities in Pittsburgh have been drawing to a close, its stock photography library is still active, and many of the images in this book can be seen at www.pittsburghscape.com. You can contact either photographer by e-mailing joellevinson@pittsburghscape.com or calling 800-782-6559. See page 104 for more about Joel and Sue.

Additional contributors to this book were John Beale and Annie O'Neill – both photographers with the *Pittsburgh Post Gazette*, Norm Schumm, Dan Amerson, Drew Levinson, and Rich Kolson.

Special thanks to the Pennsylvania Room of the Carnegie Library and the Hillman Library photographic collection for the old photographs of Pittsburgh used in this book.

Robert Gangewere, editor of *Carnegie Magazine*, wrote the original introduction and many of the captions in our first photo essay, *Pittsburgh: Views between the Rivers* (1991). However, over the years some of the introduction, captions, and headings were modified as well as new ones added by Joel B. Levinson to reflect the city as it was changing.

The driving force behind this book, and all those preceding it, was Joel's wife, Toba, to whom this latest edition is dedicated with everlasting love.

Joel B. Levinson

Susan L. Nega

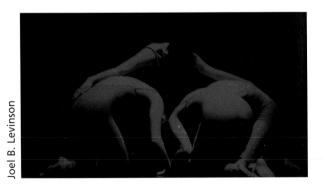

A Personal Note

Beginning in the late 1970s, I devoted many hours to gathering interesting images of Pittsburgh, images that spoke to the viewer of my city's dynamics, both from a structural standpoint and on a person-to-person interactive basis.

The images came together first in 1981 when I worked with Lynn Johnson on a black-and-white photographic essay entitled *Pittsburgh Moments*, funded by the Pittsburgh Foundation and published by University of Pittsburgh Press. I shot more than 10,000 images, and my love affair with the city was initiated. It soon became almost an obsession.

Even after *Pittsburgh Moments* was out, the drive to capture on film the wonderfully photogenic Pittsburgh landscape and splendors, the attractions, major events, and the people who make it such a wonderfully friendly, exciting city was insatiable. In 1984 Sue Nega joined me as an apprentice. Her eye was so discriminating that the imagery she captured was compelling in its creativity. Together we continued to capture the city's likenesses until 1999, when she moved on to other venues, and I planned for my own departure from a place I'd called home all my life. Even now when I'm back in the "burg," I wander the streets with my camera and hardly ever come back to the mountains around Boulder without a few rolls to be processed.

While selecting images for this essay, I passed over many I've always been partial to. The photograph of the dancers on this page was originally cut from the book, but on this page, which is somewhat more personal, it fits well.

Joel B. Levinson
April 2004